Panic-Free Public Speaking
Deliver with Confidence in 7 Simple Steps.

By Edward London-Lane

GW00382068

Clear, concise and practical. An indispensable read and guide for anyone who finds themselves in front of audiences, large or small. I've been speaking publicly for 30 odd years and wish I had had this at my side all those years ago! Whether you are new to speaking in public or a seasoned speaker, this really is a 'must read'.

Stephen Phillips, Chief Executive, China-Britain Business Council

As a teacher, being able to speak in front of others is obviously a really important skill. I felt confident with the children, however when speaking to large groups of parents and peers, I lacked the skills to be able to articulate myself. This book gave really useful tips and advice. Now I feel able to present with confidence.

R. Scott, Teacher

Table of Contents

About the Author

Edward is a speaker, coach and facilitator of communication and personal impact training in the UK and Ireland. He works closely with trainee doctors, lawyers, teachers, actors and corporate clients, nurturing public speaking, linguistics and interpersonal skills. He believes passionately that authentic communication is at the heart of all good relationships at every level. Edward lives in London with his family.

@EdLondonLane

Introduction

Answer this question: Are you a terrible Public Speaker?

And when I say terrible I mean truly awful. The worst. A stuttering wreck barely audible, sweating, crying, shaking and lost for words. If the answer is yes I challenge you. Really? *That* bad? If the answer is still yes then I question why you find yourself speaking publicly in the first place. Do you have to? Are you in the right job? Is there another position that you're more suited to instead? This may sound harsh but the reality is it's perfectly feasible to go through life leaving this rather stressful experience to others and concentrating on your strengths instead. And there's no shame in that.

If, however, the answer is 'yes I'm really that bad and no I can't leave this to someone else' then not to worry – this book will help you. Hopefully the answer is 'no I'm not terrible I just need more confidence', or 'I need help dealing with nerves', or 'I need people to engage more with what I'm saying.'

Whatever your answer, in order to get the most out of this book and to truly improve you'll need to be *honest* with yourself from the outset. Excellent public speaking requires no room for self-doubt. You need to highlight your strengths and iron-out your weaknesses so you have no 'Achilles heel', leaving you confident and comfortable in any public speaking situation.

Still on board? Good. So lets get started.

How can this book help me?

> *Fear is the main source of superstition.... To conquer fear is the beginning of wisdom.*
> *Bertrand Russell*

Professional positions often carry with them leadership responsibilities. Perhaps you find yourself having to inform staff, colleagues or the general public about process, protocol, vision, updates or forthcoming changes. You may be called upon to recruit, persuade, challenge, reprimand, encourage, pacify and inspire. In short, whether addressing a client one-to-one or a conference of thousands, an ability to communicate dynamically and effectively is paramount.

This book is designed to help you eliminate anxiety, fear and the sense of panic that arises when faced with these speaking tasks. This is not just a reading book. It's not a two-page quick fix list either. As a professional you no doubt understand the need to invest. You'll need to invest time and energy into this process applying the knowledge in this book *practically*.

Starting at the core of your relationship with speaking, you'll work through the entire process by observing your current techniques and building on them. Each step takes you closer to achieving your (Panic-Free) optimal performance, empowering you to deliver your message dynamically and achieve your objective with ease.

How do I use this book?

> *How wonderful it is that nobody need wait a single moment before starting to improve the world.*
> *Anne Frank*

As with any book, the temptation to skip to the juicy bits may only lead to frustration when the given advice doesn't 'work'. When working with clients I always tackle things in a specific order. Dealing with negative issues at the beginning (that will only continue to arise if ignored) is the best way to ensure a smooth process and ultimately - success. Therefore work through in order. Start with Step 1 and work steadily to Step 7. Some areas may feel more relevant to you than others and that's fine, you'll be guided through and advised where to move on when necessary.

Read it twice. Don't be put off if something doesn't make sense straight away, read it twice before moving on. The key to confidence can sometimes be a tiny adjustment in technique, so don't rush and risk missing out on a valuable piece of technical information.

Do the tasks. Each step has numerous tasks included. Do complete them. By treating this book as a course you'll be able to really pinpoint the areas that need attention and monitor your progress. Keep a journal or notepad so your notes are all in one place for quick reference.

Enjoy the process. Rome wasn't built in a day – cheesy but true. All new techniques take time and practice so be patient and compassionate with yourself as you work. That said you'd be amazed how the smallest adjustment can make a massive impact on your speaking ability, your confidence – and your audience experience, so experiment and play with these techniques as you learn them.

Step 1: Assess your starting point.

> *Accept everything about yourself - I mean everything, You are you
> and that is the beginning and the end - no apologies, no regrets.*
> *Henry A. Kissinger*

In order to work towards a realistic goal it's important to assess your
current level of ability. Past experiences, natural affinity and
confidence levels make each person's start level unique. However
it's important to remember – a speaker's ability is subjective.
Audiences have personal taste so there is no definitive good or bad.

Let's start with your own intuition, how good you *feel* you are.
Answer the questions below:

What are your strengths?
Remembering to be *honest* take a moment to list the areas you feel
confident in already. It could be:

Your knowledge of subject matter
Your ability to speak honestly
Your ability to maintain confident eye contact
Your passion for the topic being discussed
Your love of serving people
Your friendly, clear or commanding voice
Your extensive vocabulary
…even your dress sense

There will <u>always</u> be something you are good at.

TASK: (10 mins) Write down your list of strengths and keep this list
to hand – we'll be using it later.

What are your weaknesses?

Compile a second list, this time focusing on those areas you consider weak. Where is your confidence lacking? What areas fill you with dread? What is letting you down? Remember, be *honest*. Don't put yourself down for the sake of it. Areas could include:

Your inability to structure a speech
The sound of your voice
Your inability to speak clearly or loudly
The lack of knowledge of your subject
Fear that you are boring
Fear that you are being overly factual
Fear that you are not engaging enough.
Fear that you are trying too hard.

TASK: (10 mins) Make a note of your weaknesses and keep the list to hand.

What are your hang-ups?

This question may require you to think back through your experience of public speaking and locate anything that has left a negative imprint. In short, *have you ever had a bad experience when Public Speaking*? It could be one awful experience or a string of smaller ones. It could be a careless comment someone made to you as a child. Nothing is too small. If after serious reflection the answer is *no* then great, move on. If the answer is *yes* then complete the tasks below.

TASK: (10 mins) Write down your bad speaking experiences. We'll call these your 'hang-ups'.

TASK: (20 mins) Pick a hang-up and write a paragraph about it. Describe it in as much painful detail as possible:

Where did it happen?
When was it?

What were you wearing?
Who was there?
How did you feel?
Who witnessed it?
What was their reaction?
What was the outcome?

Go deeper:

What were you doing before it?
What did you do afterwards?
How prepared were you?
Did anyone say anything to you about it afterwards?

Once the whole awful experience has been relived complete the next task.

TASK: (20 mins) Defend yourself. Write down:

Any deciding factors why it happened.
What positive insights, knowledge or good came from it?
Why you'll never let it happen again.
What steps you'll take to ensure it never happens again.

Don't stop until you've said everything you can on the matter.

NOTE: Before advancing repeat the exercise with each of your hang-ups until the list is empty.

This will undoubtedly be the key to your success. I repeat:

> *'Excellent public speaking requires no room for self-doubt.'*

Ok, so now we've confronted past demons and have a clearer picture of where you're starting from, lets find out where you'd like to get to.

Set your Goal

> *What we call the beginning is often the end. And to make an end is to make a beginning. The end is where we start from.*
> *T. S. Eliot*

In order to achieve your optimum level of success we must first define what that success looks like to you. Everyone's needs are different. It's not enough to say 'I want to be a better public speaker' without defining what qualities 'better' entails. Give some thought to this. What *exactly* are you hoping to achieve by the end of this 7-step course?

An effective way to pinpoint excellent public speaker qualities is seeking inspiration from others. Role models could include activists, politicians, actors, presenters or people you know and work with. Qualities could include:

They are likable
They appear honest
They are passionate
They are inspirational
They ooze confidence
They own the stage physically
They have a clear and expressive voice
They are understated yet create an impact
They have a no-nonsense approach
They are warm and welcoming

You may be familiar with the popular TED Talks videos? These are an excellent source of inspiration. Why not watch a few and look for good examples?

TASK: (5 mins) Choose a person who has excellent public speaking ability. What qualities do you admire in them most? Pick the 3 top qualities and write them down.

TASK: (5 mins) Personalise each of your chosen qualities by adding them to the end of this sentence:

'When public speaking I …'

So for example if one of the chosen qualities is 'they ooze confidence' then your sentence becomes 'When public speaking *I* ooze confidence.'

I suggest you also add the following objectives to your list:
'When public speaking I *enjoy delivering the speech.*'
'When public speaking I *serve my audience well.*'

These extra two are essential when giving any speech. By striving to enjoy your speech and to serve your audience you're ensuring both parties' needs are met.

These new sentences are now your personal objectives – the definition of your success. Lets call them your *5 Core Objectives* – your mantras before you give any speech.

Set a time frame.

> *Better three hours too soon than a minute too late.*
> *William Shakespeare*

According to Parkinson's Law *'work expands so as to fill the time available for its completion'*. In other words a task will take the length of time you give to it, suggesting why most personal development items remain on the 'to-do' list because without a set completion date in place they never get completed.

Lets pick an actual date to complete your training. Do you have an event coming up where you'll be speaking? If not, can you create one?

TASK: (5 mins) Set your completion date. Be realistic - if starting from absolute beginner I suggest allowing a week per step as a guideline. If you're simply brushing up or trouble-shooting specific areas then it could be as little as a few weeks in total. Write it in your diary. Commit to it. Tell someone your date as this provides external support and it's nice to have someone to inform 'how the big day went.'

Done? Great. Now we know what you're aiming to achieve, lets get on with it.

Move on to Step 2.

Step 2: Prepare your speech

> *Success depends upon previous preparation,*
> *and without such preparation there is sure to be failure.*
> *Confucius*

When preparing your speech its important to remember, it's exactly that – *a speech*. Don't over think this part. You're not writing an essay, journal or novel. Structure certainly is important – vital in fact – but the human element can accidentally be edited out by obsessing with grammar, academic jargon and complex sentence structure. I'm sure we'd all like to be Martin Luther King, but the reality is we don't always need to be.

What format should I choose?

Whether you decide to write out your speech in full or create a series of keywords/bullet points is up to you. There are pros and cons of each and I advise trying both to see which approach serves you best.

Written Speeches.

Pros. Having your speech in written format enables you to craft it quite specifically. It leaves nothing to chance and ensures you never get stuck for words.

Cons. Hearing someone *read* a speech is less impressive than hearing someone *deliver* a speech. If you read out your speech there will be less eye contact with the audience. You may also miss the opportunity for spontaneity. If you learn the speech and recite it you risk forgetting bits or 'drying'.

NOTE: If you have your speech prepared for you it's *always* beneficial to personalise and make the speech your own.

Working from Keywords/Bullet Points

Pros. Many people prefer working from a list of structured bullet points to use as stepping-stones and guidance throughout the speech. The benefit is it enables the speaker to retain a more natural tone and adapt to the audience's response.

Cons. The drawback to working from bullet points is it provides less of a visual safety blanket should you lose your way or go blank. However regular practice will help prevent this from happening.

Both styles require exactly the same preparation regardless. I advise experimenting first to see which approach suits you best and then try a third option (my preferred approach) of creating a list of bullet points *from* your written speech.

Start simple and build as you go.

Lets start with some essential groundwork before we structure the speech itself.

TASK: (20 mins) As concisely and accurately as possible, write down your answers to the following *Ground Work Questions*:

What's your objective?

What do you want the end result to be?
What do you want people to go away feeling, thinking or doing as a result of your speech?

What's your message?

What core message are you aiming to get across during this speech? By this I mean the actual facts, the essential information that needs to be imparted – your reason for being here.

Who are they?

Who are your audience?
Why are they here?
What are they hoping, needing or wanting to hear?

Are you about to give them what they want or not?

Align your message with your audience's needs – how does it effect them?

Who are you?

Why are you standing in front of us right now?

What do you do?

What strengths do you already have to help deliver this speech? Refer back to your list of strengths.

How might you need to adapt your style in order to best connect with your audience?

What approach might you use?

CHECK IN: That's the hard work done. These answers are the core of your speech. Stay true to all of them and you can't really go wrong. Famous last words? Not really. *True confidence when Public Speaking comes from feeling secure with your message, your audience's expectations and your personal objective.* All other elements are useful extras that simply add shape, texture and colour.

TASK: (45 mins max) Write your speech right now using only the information from your *Ground Work Questions*. It will feel a bit dry, factual and non-dynamic but that's totally fine at this stage.

Add-Ons:

Only once you've done your groundwork draft can you afford to start 'adding on' useful extras. Remember we're still working on the *content* of the speech at this point, not the spoken delivery of it – that comes later, but this vital preparation will make a successful delivery infinitely more possible.

Work through the Add-Ons below and apply the relevant elements to make your speech more dynamic.

I've broken the Add-Ons areas into three sections:

Section 1: Impact Points

Section 2: Audience Extras
Section 3: Opening/Q&A/Closing

Section 1: Impact points. These are elements within your speech that create an impact on the listener. They engage the audience, turning them from passive listeners into active listeners and evoke emotional responses like surprise, interest, and amusement or provoke debate.

Facts. You can't argue with a fact. It's unemotional and is a useful starting point for discussion. Try using a surprising one (relevant to your topic of course) that will get a reaction from the audience. People love finding out new things – especially amazing things.

TASK: (5 mins) Gather some useful facts. A useful resource for this is Google. Simple type in 'facts about…(your topic)'

Questions. Engage your audience by making them think. Pose them a question and leave a few beats of silence. It provokes an opinion or emotional response. Don't feel the need to answer all questions immediately either. A hypothetical question leaves space for you to explore possible answers as you go along.

Active Questions. To get an audience invested in the speech try using an active question. This makes them physically answer it: 'Who here has ever been to Spain? Let me see a show of hands.' Or 'Stand up if you've ever received bad service at a restaurant. Ok, now remain standing if you ever went back there again?' By getting the audience physically involved you not only activate them but also provide a visual to help illustrate your point.

TASK: (10 mins) Think of a question or active question you could pose to your audience at the start of your speech to get them thinking about your main topic. Write down two more questions related to your audience's needs. Add them in to your speech.

Examples. Using an example is an excellent way of backing up a statement. It proves a point or brings credibility to what you're saying. If you're mentioning the benefits of something– give us an example. If you're explaining a process to us – show us an example. Try bringing in a case study to show the impact your topic has already had on someone else. Get creative and remember examples can be spoken or visual. Spoken examples can incorporate humorous anecdotes or vibrant storytelling.

TASK: (15 mins) Look through your speech and back up all statements with an example. Choose the example and decide what the most dynamic way of presenting it is. Visual aids can also be useful. Explore using projectors and video for presenting pictures, words, graphs or films.

Storytelling. It's part of human nature to enjoy listening to stories. Use it to enliven your examples. Storytelling is not only fun for the listener but also the teller. Enjoy yourself.

TIP: To make your story dramatically interesting and concise try adopting a technique followed by storytellers and writers: *Get into your story as late as you can and get out as soon as you can.*

TASK: (10 mins) Choose a story that's relevant to the core elements of your speech. Use as many adjectives (describing words) as possible. Bring it alive with textures, colours, sights, sounds, tastes and smells.

Quotes. Quotes are an excellent way of getting your point across directly. They can be inspirational and make an impact. What's more, someone else has already done the work for you. A well-placed quote cashes in on an influential person's reputation and credibility.

TASK: (10 mins) Google quotes related to the *message* of your speech. Add it in. This will add power and gravitas to the importance of the information you have to impart.

Humour. How many of you chose 'using humour' or 'being funny' as one of your core objectives in Step 1? And perhaps rightly so – using humour can lighten even the drollest of subjects. It's a memorable skill that many excellent public speakers have. Anyone who's ever watched Sir Ken Robinson talk about education will certainly know what I'm talking about. However, the *pressure to be funny* is the one thing that is guaranteed to not only cause stress but also kill any natural humour that may already be present. *Don't focus on being funny.* It's an art form in itself and, unless you're already a natural comedian, release yourself from this burden right now. But that's not to say you *won't be* funny. Often a relaxed throwaway comment said with a smile is all it takes to get people on your side.

TASK: Let go of any pressure to be funny. However, if a joke comes to mind when you're structuring your speech then put it in. You can see how it's received when you practice later on.

Statements of Passion. Don't be afraid to include passionate statements. Being genuinely enthusiastic is inspirational and enthuses the audience. Be inventive with your adjectives and avoid bland or generic words like *great, good, amazing* and *nice.*

TASK: (10 mins) Look for opportunities within your speech to include passionate language. Upgrade any bland statements or words into something more driven.

Section 2: Audience extras: Consider your audience in more detail:

Cultural Differences. Are there any cultural differences to bear in mind? People from certain cultures respond better to a more direct approach. Eastern Europeans, Scandinavians and Chinese for example don't respond well to small talk and niceties. Other cultures are more indirect. British and Japanese feel more at ease with friendly rapport building and etiquette.

Status. What is the status of your audience? Are they peers for example? Are they executives? Does their experience in your topic exceed your own or are they beginners?

Jargon. What terminology is going to make your messages most accessible? Are you speaking their language? Can you reduce any jargon?

Formality. Consider the formality that would best suit your audience. Is it an informal and relaxed affair that lends itself to light-hearted anecdotes and slang, or is it a more formal event with gravitas and a higher sense of ceremony?

Task vs. Relationship. If it's more important to build a better *relationship with your audience* then reduce the use of facts and figures and focus more on what's important to your audience's needs. If the *information* within the speech is more important then highlight it by repeating the key message and explain how failing to retain this information may impact upon them.

TASK: (30 mins) Refer back to the your *Ground Work Questions*. Are there any facts about your audience that you can bear in mind? Tailor your speech to fit their tastes and needs?

Section 3: Opening. Avoid lengthy explanations outlining what you're intending to talk about or what led you to this point in time. Engaging an audience from the very beginning requires you to get them actively thinking. Jump straight in with something relevant and powerful. Then bring *them* into the equation as soon as possible.

TASK: (15 mins) Follow this format and see if it works for your speech: Open with a fact or quote.
Follow with a rhetorical question – challenge them.

Introduce a relevant inspirational story to highlight the points you're about to make and prove your connection to your topic.

Once you have them gripped you can get more specific about the reason you are here.

Now explain how this is relevant to them and the impact it will have on them.

Q & A. Whilst by no means always necessary, offering a question and answer session at the end of the speech shows confidence in your field of expertise. It also allows your audience to feel like their opinions are being heard. However, having a Q&A session does risk your speech ending on a note determined by someone else. Another option is to state at some point during the speech (not the end) that you'd be happy to have a quick chat afterwards with anyone who has questions.

TASK: (10 mins) If you *do* plan a Q&A consider what questions may be asked and have an idea what your answers would be.

Closing. The closing of your speech is what you'll ultimately be judged on. Those final words and images are what the audience remembers most so make them count. Sum up briefly, tying together everything you've covered but avoid using the words 'in conclusion' – be a bit more inventive.

TASK: Choose a quote that sums up the speech's message or invite the audience to ponder upon another rhetorical question. Then, keeping your objective in mind, inspire them to take action. Once you've done so – finish on a high. Don't fizzle out.

Remember – *what you say last is what the audience will remember most.*

The Practice Draft:

In any form of writing a first draft is always awful and requires redrafting. Your speech will be no different. Leave it for a hour/day or two and return with a fresh pair of eyes. Read it out aloud (always) and note down any areas that stick in your throat or feel over/under written. Rewrite it. Don't be precious, just do it and it will almost certainly be better. Do this two or three times.

Editorial Tips:

Don't info dump. Good speakers make the effort to edit their content beforehand and deliver only the choice cuts to their audience. Choose your words mindfully – less is more so be *selective*. Find ways of saying things with as few words as possible.

TASK: (15 mins) Work through your speech and edit out any unnecessary words or unrelated pieces of information.

Definite language. If the intention of your speech is to influence or persuade your audience then beware of using overly 'definite' language. Words like; *will, are, is, do, definitely, certainly* etc can be received as pushy and leave little room for personal opinion or choice. By introducing the idea of 'possibility' into you language by using words like; *perhaps, could, maybe, sometimes, if, occasionally* etc you offer your audience the space to make up their own minds or 'buy in' to your idea. If the intention of your speech is to motivate your audience then definite language is perfect - adding that little push.

TASK: (15 mins) Check the 'definite' vocabulary you're using in your speech. Does it suit your intention in terms of the impact you want on your audience?

Magic three. This is an age-old literary trick. Putting things in examples of three is attractive to the ear, interesting to the mind and just sounds right. See?

TASK: (15 mins) Look through your speech and find an opportunity to add in the Magic Three.

Assumptive Statements. Avoid assumptive statements like *no doubt you will…* or *you're probably thinking…* or *I'm sure you know...* These can alienate members of your audience you *don't* already know, or encourage them to disagree out of principal.

TASK: (5 mins) Look through your speech and remove any assumptive statements.

Use of Pronouns. Take a few minutes to observe which pronouns you've chosen to include. Pronouns play a big part in how *engaged* your audience are.

'We' – Using *we* in a sentence only really works if you've already set up an *I, you, us* context. Without this the word *we* becomes rather metaphorical and removed, enabling the audience to take a back seat and disengage. '*We*' never takes action – '*you*' do. If you're talking peer-to-peer then *we* is inclusive and works well, however if you're in management and addressing staff or the public then *we* sets up an *us and them* context – creating a divide.

'I' – Be certain to use the word *I* to show the audience how engaged you are with what you're saying. It personalises your speech, makes them hear a human speaking rather than a formal script.

'You' – Addressing the audience as *you* makes a connection with them. It makes it personal and invites them to have an opinion.

'One' – Using one instead of *I, you* or *we* is very formal. Personally I would avoid it or think seriously about what tone you're trying to achieve first.

TASK: (15 mins) Revisit your pronouns and ensure they encourage full engagement at all times.

Main aim. Being conscious of the *main aim* of the speech helps you make choices when choosing the content. Are you:

Giving instructions?
Influencing? (selling)
Delivering Information?
Sharing a vision?

It's likely to be a combination of the above but try to define which is the dominant aim.

TASK: (15 mins) Work through your speech and underline each sentence that directly links to your main aim. If the majority of your sentences don't then see if you can readdress the balance by adapting sentences to serve it better.

Once you have your speech - let someone else read it. Again choose your reader wisely – someone who knows your topic or works with you. At this stage it's still a draft that can be changed as you practice, but it's useful to get initial feedback.

Congratulations! You now have your speech. The content is structured to serve both you and your audience, and it has a secure message and an objective you can trust.

Move on to Step 3.

Step 3: Basic Vocal Warm ups

> *Physical fitness is not only one of the most important keys to a healthy body, it is the basis of dynamic and creative intellectual activity.*
> *John F. Kennedy*

Just as an athlete regularly warms-up before a race, so to must any professional whose job requires public speaking. Or they should. An *'it'll be alright on the night'* approach seldom works and often leads to disappointment or a damaging experience that can take years to undo. Actors, singers, politicians, presenters, musicians, CEO's and commentators all regularly practice vocal techniques in order to have the confidence and skill needed to do their job professionally. Start practicing now. Vocal exercises are often extremely simple and can be done in minutes. Just 10 minutes each day can dramatically improve your vocal quality, breath control and clarity of speech.

Below is a list of exercises. Each one explains what area it develops and how to do it. Start the habit of practicing them daily – in the shower, driving the car, at home or at the office.

I have arranged them in 3 sections:
Section 1 – Warming up physically
Section 2 – Activating your breath and support muscles
Section 3 – Warming up vocally

Section 1: Warming Up Physically
All muscles need some physical effort to warm them up. Simple stretches are a great way to start. I encourage you to stretch the entire body but at the very least concentrate on the neck, shoulder and facial muscles.

The following exercises gently loosen the neck muscles.

Neck
Exercise 1 – Head turns. Keeping your upper body still, simply alternate looking left and right slowly. Repeat 5 times.

Exercise 2 – Head tilts. Facing the front, drop your head sideways towards your shoulder. Lift back to starting position. Repeat on the other side. Repeat whole exercise 5 times.

NOTE: Do not push the head. Allow its natural weight to stretch the neck.

Exercise 3 – Head rolls. Drop your chin to your chest and gently roll the head over to one shoulder. Now roll it to the other shoulder. Repeat twice. Now roll the head all the way round slowly, making sure you open your mouth when the head is laying back to stop any strain on your throat. Repeat, rolling the other way. Lift head back to the start position.

The following exercises gently loosen the shoulder muscles.

Shoulders
Exercise 1 – Shoulder roll. Roll your shoulders forwards five times. Now roll them backwards five times.

Exercise 2 – Arm swing. Gently swing your arms (straight) forwards five times. Now swing them backwards five times.

Exercise 3 – Ceiling stretch. Raise both arms straight above your head. Take it in turns to stretch one hand higher than the other. (This also stretches the rib muscles, which is helpful for breath control.)

The following exercises gently loosen the tongue, jaw and facial muscles.

Face

Exercise 1 – Face Rub. Give yourself a vigorous face rub all over with your fingers. Don't forget your eyes, eyebrows, cheeks, lips, ears, forehead and chin.

Exercise 2 – Small face/Big face. Scrunch your face up tightly. Hold for a few seconds and release. Now make a 'big face' by open your mouth widely with tongue out and eyes wide. Hold for a few seconds and release. Repeat five times.

Exercise 3 – Toffee chew. Imagine you have a large, hard toffee in your mouth. So large you can't close your mouth. Start to 'work the toffee' by biting down on it in small movements. Feel your jaw muscles start to work. Imagine the toffee getting softer and more supple as you chew. Now imagine it is very soft and work the toffee around your mouth. Swallow. Now use your tongue to clean every tooth in your mouth, front, back and in between.

Exercise 4 – Yawn. Simply encourage yourself to yawn. Yawning is excellent for releasing throat tension and stretching the soft palate (a useful part of the throat when speaking.)

Exercise 5 – Thumb rub. Allow your jaw to drop open loosely and your tongue to relax fully. Now use both thumbs to make a 'thumbs up' sign. Place your thumbs under your chin, behind the jaw bone (all of the above flesh is your tongue muscle.) Gently massage upwards keeping the tongue fully relaxed.

NOTE: This is an excellent tongue warm-up but can make some people gag or feel queasy. Do it if you can.

Exercise 6 – Tongue stretch. Stick your tongue out. Explore each direction (up, down, left, right and circle round) without moving your head or jaw. Repeat several times.

Exercise 7 – Jaw stroke. Relax you jaw open. Using the fleshy bit on the palms of your hands, gently stroke your jaw downwards five times.

Exercise 8 – Jaw socket. Using your thumbs, locate your jaw sockets either side at the top of your jawbone, below your cheekbones. (You'll know you've found the right spot when your thumbs are pushed outwards when you open and close your jaw) Gently press in and massage these sockets.

Exercise 9 – Jaw shake. Clasp you hands together. Touch your elbows together too. Allow your jaw to hang loosely. Now shake your clasped hands forwards and backwards vigorously whilst letting out a small groan. If your jaw is nice and loose it will bounce up and down and you'll sound like you're going over bumpy ground. If there is jaw tension the sound will not change.

Section 2: Activating your breath and support muscles.

Good breath control is vital for good public speaking. Not only is it necessary to enable a balanced, flowing delivery but it also plays a key role in dealing with nerves and tension.
Whilst each of us breathes naturally without giving it a second thought, learning to control breath is actually quite hard and can take years of practice. Don't let this put you off. Some simple exercises can make a vast improvement in very little time at all.

The following exercises aim to develop breath control.

Note: It's perfectly normal to feel a little light-headed when performing vocal exercises that you're not used too. If at any point you feel light-headed, stop and breathe normally for a few minutes.

Exercise 1 – Low breathing. Most people naturally breath high up in their chests. This limits the amount of breath you can take in and often creates tension in the upper body. Our aim here is to start training the body to breath lower down into the stomach area. Place your hands on your stomach. Without pushing, gently breathe in through your nose and send the breath down towards your hands. Let go of the stomach muscles and allow the area to push outwards. Repeat at your own pace. See if you can keep your chest and shoulders still and allow only your hands to move.

Exercise 2 – Ping-pong blow. This is a simple yet excellent breath control exercise. Using the same *low breathing* technique, breathe in for four counts, hold for four counts and breathe out for four counts. When breathing out imagine you are blowing a ping-pong ball across a table at chin height. Try to keep the flow of air steady enough for the ball to reach the end of the table at the end of the counts. Repeat this a few times. Now try the exercise to an exhale of eight counts. Again concentrate on a steady jet of airflow. Gently build the length of the exhale over time.

Exercise 3 – Shush! Place closed fists either side of your waist just below the ribcage. Using low breathing, inhale for four counts, hold for four counts and exhale on a 'Shhhhh' sound until all your breath has been released. Repeat, this time sending short bursts of 'Sh! Sh! Sh! Sh!' until your breath has gone. Imagine you are blowing out a candle each time. This exercise engages your *support* muscles, which are the foundation for solid speech. When performed correctly, you'll notice your fists being kicked outwards slightly by your muscles. This may take time but keep practicing.

Exercise 4 – Funny. This is a variation on exercise 3 and also gets your *support* muscles working. Place the fingers of your right hand just below your belly button. Now place the fingers of your left hand just above your belly button. Using low breathing, inhale for four counts, hold for four counts and exhale on short bursts of 'Ha! Ha! Ha! Ha!' until your breath has gone. When performed correctly your left hand (above) should kick outwards and your right hand (below) should kick inwards. The movement is slight but definite. Once again, it may take time to perfect but keep practicing this one.

Section 3: Warming Up Vocally

Once the muscles are warm and the breath is engaged, it's time to start warming up our vocal chords and articulating our tongue and lips.

The following exercises gently warms-up the vocal chords and flexes the vocal range.

Exercise 1 – Siren. Gently hum, making an 'Mmmmm' sound. Explore sliding the pitch up and down like a police siren. See how high and low you can go. Repeat a few times.

NOTE: Don't push this, let it be natural and see if you can engage your support muscles. (Put your fists on your sides as in the 'Shush' exercise to test it out.) Also don't stretch your neck up or down during the exercise.

Exercise 2 – Siren 2. Repeat the above exercising using the 'ng' sound found at the end of the word 'sing'.

Exercise 3 – Freezing! This exercise is incredibly effective when warming up the vocal chords and needs very relaxed lips to work properly. Imagine you're cold and making a 'brrrrr!' sound. Siren up and down with it several times.

Exercise 4 – Rolled R. Place the tip of your tongue behind your top teeth. Blow air through your mouth and say the word 'red'. If you can roll your R's easily try a siren at the same time.

The following exercises develop diction and clarity by focusing on consonants and vowel sounds.

Exercise 1 – BDGD. This exercise uses the lower-case sounds of these letters (buh, duh, guh, duh) to work the lips, the tongue and the soft palate. Keeping the letters in order (b, d, g, d), repeat them slowly as clearly as possible. Once you have mastered the pattern try picking up the pace a bit (bdgd, bdgd, bdgd, bdgd) without losing clarity.

Exercise 2 – PTKT. This is actually the same exercise as above but with the 'voice' taken away. This means we are doing the same thing but without engaging our vocal folds. An easier way to visualise it is by replacing BDGD with the lower case sound of PTKT (puh, tuh, kuh, tuh). Again start the sequence slowly, repeating until you can pick up the pace.

Exercise 3 – BDGD/PTKT. Feeling confident? Try building up to alternating the two.

Exercise 4 – MNMNMN. This exercise works the lips and tip of the tongue. Simply alternate the sound of the letters M and N ('muh' and 'nuh') over and over again. Build speed and clarity.

Exercise 5 – Vowels & Endings. In order to speak clearly and be fully understood, it's important not to drop the end consonant of a word. This exercise trains the mouth to finish words crisply and clearly. Learn the following sequence:

Oo (as in WHO)
Oh (as in SO)
Aw (as in SAW)
Ah (as in BAR)
Ay (as in DAY)
Ee (as in SEE)

Choose a consonant (a non-vowel) and add it to the end of each sound in the sequence. For example, if we choose 'P' the sequence would become:

Oo**p**
Oh**p**
Aw**p**

Ah**p**
Ay**p**
Ee**p**

Repeat the sequence with at least another five different consonants.

Exercise 6 – Tongue Twister. The following excerpt, taken from Robert Browning's Pied Piper of Hamlyn, is excellent for practicing vocal clarity. See how much colour, diction and clarity you can infuse it with:

Rats!
They fought the dogs and killed the cats,
And bit the babies in the cradles,
And ate the cheeses out of the vats,
And licked the soup from the cooks' own ladles,
Split open the kegs of salted sprats,
Made nests inside men's Sunday hats,
And even spoiled the women's chats,
By drowning their speaking
With shrieking and squeaking
In fifty different sharps and flats.

Exercise 7 – Tongue-out Twister. Repeat the above excerpt with your tongue sticking out. Try to be as clear and precise as possible. Now repeat the tongue twister normally and notice the difference.

Disclaimer: I can in no way be held responsible for any injury obtained as a result of the misuse or following of these exercises. Always consult a doctor if you have any doubt before starting the exercises. These simple vocal and physical exercises are universally known and have been tried and tested by thousands of speakers with excellent results in many different professions. Be gentle with your body.

Challenge yourself and commit to a daily physical and vocal warm up.
Visit www.publicspeaking7steps.com for your FREE audio **10-minute Vocal Maximiser**.

Move on to Step 4.

Step 4: Discover Your Current Habits.

> *We are what we repeatedly do. Excellence, then, is not an act, but a habit.*
> *Aristotle*

Everyone's speech and movement patterns are unique. Characteristics are picked up and developed throughout a lifetime; some are family traits, some are personal choices and others a result of circumstance, geography and environment.

Discovering your own current performance habits is a vital part of your progress. Some will serve you well, others will not and some may need a tweak in the right direction to make your performance more effective. In order to do this we must first observe and self-analyse your current style.

NOTE: This kind of personal analysis is almost always an uncomfortable experience. Rest assured that it's perfectly natural to cringe when seeing yourself on camera and that *no one* likes the sound of their own voice. However, this needs to be overcome for a brief instance in order to gather stock of where your current performance level lies.

I have split this into two sections:
Section 1: Self-Analysis
Section 2: External Analysis

Section 1: Self-Analysis
Live filming
The easiest way to start this process is to film yourself giving a speech. *In situ* is ideal as it gives an accurate account of how you currently perform in front of an audience.

TASK: Set up a camera discretely at the back of the room, press the record button and then forget about it. Filming from far away will illustrate how your speech is received right at the back of the room. This approach is better than someone holding a phone up in the audience as that may put you off.

Demo-speech filming
If you're not in a position to record live speeches then a demo-speech is the next best thing.

TASK: (5-15 mins) Set up a camera at the back of a room and imagine giving your speech to a room full of people. Always enter and exit the space and practice in full-voice, with total commitment.

NOTE: Avoid making the speech too long. The purpose is to use it as a case study. A 5-10 minute speech is perfect as you will be playing it back many times.

These films are for you to review and analyse.

Reviewing the footage. What am I looking for?
At this stage we're *simply looking to see what's there.* If you were perfect already (and nobody is) then you wouldn't be reading this book, so don't feel downhearted at what you see. The objective here is to give yourself constructive criticism and improve any areas you feel are lacking.

TASK: (Take your time with this. It will mean watching your speech video many times so spread it out over a few days.) Imagine you're watching a good friend who's asked you to observe and feedback on their public speaking skills. Watch your speech and write these observations down, being as specific as you can. Use the list of *'elements that effect communication'* below to help you. Be as accurate and compassionate as possible. The areas to look at are:

What's being said.

How it's being said.
What's not being said. (body language)

NOTE: The objective at this stage is simply to list the areas that need work. Don't over think it or beat yourself up.

We will address how to improve these areas in Steps 5 & 6.

Below is a list of areas to analyse your speech with. Not all of them will apply so don't be overwhelmed but do work through them all.

Elements that effect communication and should be considered are:

Pitch/speed/volume

<u>Pitch</u> - We've already established that everyone's voice is different. Some sit higher up in the vocal register and others lower. Some are more resonant and others less so. There is no 'perfect' pitch when it comes to speaking, but it's often useful to experiment and notice the result.

TASK: (5 mins) Where does your voice naturally sit in terms of pitch? Listen to your recording and note what affect this has on your speech.

<u>Speed</u> – Whatever your natural speaking speed, a dose of nerves always has an impact. The desire to *get it over with* can speed up a speech and make it too fast for the audience to follow. This can also lead to mumbling, tripping over words and lack of breath control. Alternatively it can have the opposite effect, leaving the speaker slow, stilted and looking like a rabbit in headlights.

TASK: (5 mins) Mark your speed from 1 (slow) to 10 (fast). What is the impact of that on your speech?

<u>Volume</u> – If you use a microphone this may not be an issue, but if you're speaking without then observe how loud you are. If, having filmed yourself from the back of a room, you can hear every word – then move on - there isn't much of an issue. If you can't hear everything then:

TASK: (10 mins) Note down where in the speech your vocal level drops. Is it at the end of sentences? Is it during your humorous, throwaway comments? Is it at the start due to nerves or at the end due to a desire to finish? Are you looking down too often and losing words as a result? Write it all down.

Stresses.

Stresses create a dynamic impact within a sentence. This can be useful when highlighting an important point, but if used incorrectly they can change how the listener interprets the message.

For example: Imagine you are a patient in a Doctor's surgery and you hear the following sentence: 'You need to stop smoking.' The message is quite clear, right? Now replay the Doctor's message with a stress on each of the individual words and see how different the tone of each sentence sounds.

'*You* need to stop smoking.' (Accusatory)
'You *need* to stop smoking.' (Pleading)
'You need to *stop* smoking.' (Demanding)
'You need to stop *smoking*.' (Exasperated)

TASK: (10 mins) Make a note of where the stresses lie within your speech by marking them with a coloured dot. Are they being used with maximum impact to elevate your message?

NOTE: If English is your second language be extra aware of any stresses from your mother tongue that are being carried over unnecessarily into your English.

Intonation.

The importance of varied intonation is key to engaging the listener throughout. Imagine your speech written down like musical notes. This would show where your voice rises and falls in terms of *intonation*. A piece of music that consists of only one note will sound rather dull - so too will your speech.

TASK: (10 mins) Listen to your speech. Are you using enough intonation to keep listeners interested? Underline any areas that sound flat – try using a wiggly coloured line to prompt yourself to liven it up next time you read it. Good public speaking is like good storytelling it's vibrant, colourful and engaging.

Knowledge
When watching your film *does it looks like you know what you're talking about*? If not, why not? What clues can you detect that make you think this? Are you pausing too often? Do you say 'um' or 'er' a lot? Are you speaking in never-ending sentences? Are you stumbling over words often?

TASK: (10 mins) Write down these observations and mark each place you say 'um/er' with a recognisable symbol so we can address the situation later.

Structure (& Phrasing)
A well-structured speech has (at the very least) a beginning, middle and end. It stays on topic and is varied throughout with elements of humour where appropriate, colourful examples and moments of storytelling. It feels inclusive and invites the audience to think, have an opinion and learn new things.

TASK: (10 mins) Take note of which areas in your speech stand out or 'work' for you. See if you can pinpoint why that is: Are there areas that let the speech down? What is the cause of that do you think?

Unwanted Noises

'Bad habits' can present themselves in unusual ways. Nervous twitches not only develop physically but also vocally. Listen carefully for anything that shows up repeatedly. These can include:

Sighs
Tutting or lip smacking (often due to dry mouth and nerves)
Over swallowing
Throat clearing or coughing
'Um…'
'Errr…'
'Mmmm'
'Yeah?'
'Like,' – or an equivalent *encouragement* word from your local dialect (Ken, la, yo)
Nervous laughs.

Often these sounds creep in when buying time to think or when changing subjects.

TASK: (10 mins) Write down your 'go to' bad habits.

Use of silence
People's relationship with silence differs greatly. The most common tendency is to fear it and therefore fill it with a stream of talking. Some people are less conscious and allow long pregnant pauses between topics, leaving their audience hanging in mid-air.

TASK: (10 mins) Note down how often you use silence and how comfortable that silence is. What do you do during it? Are you smiling or fidgeting? Do you fill a potential silence with an unwanted noise or gesture? What is your eye contact like during your silences?

Fluency
The *flow* of a speech refers to the flow of content within each section. It also refers to how fluid the transitions between each

section of your speech are. Flow directly affects the level of engagement a speaker has with their audience. Even a well-structured speech can fall flat if not executed fluently.

TASK: (10 mins) Are your sentences too long? Do you stay on topic or wander off? Are you labouring a point? Are you being too factual? Are you boring yourself? Are you missing opportunities for story telling, humour or examples? Write down your thoughts.

Body language, Facial expression & Gesture
This is a vast topic and could easily be a separate book in itself. However don't underestimate how much you innately know on this subject. It's in our nature to read signals and decipher meaning simply by looking at someone's face and body language.

Eyes –Eye contact really is your number one communication tool. Pay particular attention to where you're looking, who you're looking at, when you look at someone and how long you hold a glance.

Face – Are you smiling? Do you bite your lips? Do you look terrified? Are you frowning?

Feet – Just like any building needs a solid foundation to stand with gravitas – so do you. Look at your feet. How grounded do you look? Are you shifting your weight from one side to the other? Do you sink in one hip? Are your feet close together or far apart? Are you pacing about?

Hands – Our hands betray us at every opportunity if we're nervous and feeling under confident. Observe what you do with yours. Are they relaxed? Are they shaking? Do you rub them, tap them or clench them? Are you holding anything like notepaper, spectacles or a pen – and if so does that help or distract?

Walk - When you enter and exit do you stride, shuffle or skulk? Do you appear eager, nervous or relaxed?

<u>Gesture</u> – Using our arms to gesture can be an asset during a speech. Observe yours. Do your arm movements look confident? Do they create a relaxed atmosphere? Are they twitchy and sporadic? Are your gestures all necessary? Do you use any at all?

TASK: (20 mins) Make a note of any body language that stands out as superfluous or distracting. We can address these in Step 6.

CHECK IN: You now have your list of *habit observations*. These point you towards the areas that need working on in steps 5 & 6.

Section 2: External Analysis

The next phase of analysis is to gather *external* feedback.

TASK: (10-30 mins) Ask a colleague or friend to watch your speech (live) and give their thoughts. (Read the advice below first.)

NOTE: It's very easy for close friends and family to be overly nice or overly critical in these situations. Choose someone whose opinion you respect, but who isn't too close and won't adapt their feedback.

Be specific about what feedback you want. For example, instead of asking 'How did I do?' ask questions like:

Could you hear every word?
Did I look relaxed?
Did you understand each point I was making?
Was there anything I did particularly well?
Was there anything that was distracting?
Did I do anything physically that looked insecure or unusual?

Ask them to write their thoughts down, or record their response so you have them to refer to. Whatever the feedback, accept their comments graciously and with interest. Always thank them and never justify or argue your case – you may need their opinion again in the future! Try using this script:

'Thank you, that's very useful feedback and has given me lots to think about and work on.'

Then leave it at that and reflect upon their comments elsewhere. Add them to your list of *Habit Observations*.

TASK: (5 mins) Have a quick re-read of your 'list of weaknesses' from Step 1. Remember these were the weaknesses you *felt* you had. Were you proved right? Or did some of your perceived weaknesses not appear in reality when you watched your speech? Were you pleasantly surprised? Cross off any weaknesses that are not actually true.

Move on to Step 5.

Step 5: Delivery Technique (Vocal)

> *Words mean more than what is set down on paper.*
> *It takes the human voice to infuse them with deeper meaning.*
> *Maya Angelou*

This next step will approach the speech vocally and get you up on your feet.

CHECK IN: From this point onwards keep your notes to hand as a guideline.
These are:
Your *5 core objectives* – i.e. to be confident, engaging, likable etc
Your list of weaknesses.
Your list of *Habit Observations*.

How to proceed through Step 5. Use the information and exercises in this step to improve the issues on your lists. Take your time and don't forget to acknowledge the elements of your voice that *are already working well*. The objective of this step isn't to create insecurities but to troubleshoot common vocal issues.

Let's begin.

How do I stop myself running out of breath?
Breath and support are key to clear delivery. Without it a speaker can sound shaky, quiet or underconfident. It can also lead to light-headedness and panic. Running out of breath is a sign of nerves or lack of support and grounding. Taking calm, deep breaths floods your body with a pleasant sensation and helps keep anxiety at bay. Make sure your feet are firmly planted on the ground with your weight evenly spread. Picture the deep breaths being sent down into your feet.

TASK: Supporting your breath provides the sturdy base to produce an even voice and ensures longevity to your vocal health. Return to the breath and support exercises in Step 3 and practice regularly. Perform the exercises before you speak on the big day.

How do I stop mumbling?

No audience member wants to struggle to hear what a speaker is saying. Making the effort to be clear is very important.

Take your time. Be sure to finish each word by hitting all end consonants.

Leave enough space between words to allow the listener to not only hear them but also digest them.

TASK: In Step 3 there were plenty of exercises to develop clarity and diction. Practice often and always do these before the speech on the day.

TASK: (5 mins) Recite the first five lines of your speech with your tongue out. Really try to speak as precisely and clearly as possible. Now repeat those lines with your tongue back in and notice the difference.

NOTE: This exercise may make some people gag. Persevere if you can – it really is effective.

How do I create a more professional sound/tone to my voice?

Professional speakers often *adapt their voice* to fit their environment, audience or subject. News Readers for example frequently alter their *vocal tone* from story to story. Actors *project* (speak louder) to fill the space. Storytellers use varied *intonation and pitch* to draw-in and engage their audience.

TASK: (5 mins) Before we address this issue, define what 'professional' means to you. What qualities are you referring too?

Each individual has a unique voice. In order to *adapt our natural tone* we must first get familiar with our current *Resonance, Placement* and *Pitch*.

Think of 'Resonance' as *the place in the body where the sound vibrations happen,* 'Placement' as *the place in the mouth where the words happen,* and 'Pitch' as *how high or low the voice sounds.* All three elements affect the voice's *tone* which is what we are attempting to adapt.

Resonance. The main areas where people resonate when speaking are the chest, throat, mouth, nose and head. Each area has its own tonal quality. Whilst none are necessarily right or wrong, concentrating purely on one area alone can sound restricted. To create a professional tone I recommend exploring a *combination of chest, mouth and nose resonance.*

TASK: (10 mins) Speak a few lines of your speech and attempt to locate where your natural *resonance* lies. Feel for the vibrations with your hands. Repeat and explore shifting the vibration to the other areas. How does that affect the quality of your voice? Did it make you sound more professional? Is one area more effective than the other? If it helped then repeat your speech, keeping the resonance in this area all the way through.

Placement. Words are formed either at the front of the mouth, the back of the mouth or anywhere in between.

Placing the voice further *back* in the mouth tends to result in a lower tone with less diction.

Placing the voice in the *middle* makes if difficult to use the tongue and lips effectively - think of speaking whilst eating a hot potato.

To create a more professional sound I recommend placing the voice more towards the *front* of the mouth. This helps with diction and clarity.

TASK: (10 mins) Stand facing a wall (a few centimetres away) and speak a few lines of your speech deliberately placing the vibration at the front of your mouth and nose. See if you can get your lips and nose tingling. Once you have achieved this sensation take a step away and *keep the placement*, imagining you are still up against the wall. Keep taking steps further away, repeating the exercise. This will not only help you with forward placement but also encourage you to project (speak loudly) and engage your support muscles.

Pitch. Sometimes nerves affect our voice's natural pitch. This can result in a low mumble or a shrill nervous squeak. Adapting your pitch may help you feel more grounded and create the professional quality you seek. Men often benefit from *raising* their pitch (i.e. making the sound higher) in order to sound more personable. This also helps the voice to carry further in a space. Actors often raise the pitch of their voices on stage. Women sometimes benefit from *lowering* their voices to add gravitas.

TASK: (10 mins) Play around with pitch. Refer back to your initial recorded speech and see if it needs tweaking. Does your voice sound more friendly and appealing if you raise the pitch? Do you feel more grounded and authoritative if you drop the pitch? Adapt to create the professional tone you desire.

How do I speak louder (project)?

Meeting the room vocally is vital. Microphones may help, but it's still best practice to learn to project your voice to the back of the space. In order to do this you'll need to engage you support muscles and ensure proper breathing. It also helps to imagine the back row as being hard of hearing.

TASK: (5 mins) Ensure you've warmed-up first using the exercises in Step 3. Take a deep breath and on the out-breath send short, sharp bursts of 'Shh!' or 'Ha!' to each chair in the back row. This engages your support and prepares your body for the level of effort needed to project during your speech. It's also a good warm up and helps you make a mental connection with the size of the space. When performed effectively, it should give you the same sensation in your stomach as when you cough.

TASK: (10 mins) Practice your speech putting a 'H' in front of each word. Attempt to achieve the same 'kick' on each word as you did in the above exercise. Imagine you are giving the speech to the back row. NOTE: Maintain the same vocal level even when looking at the people at the front.

I'm rushing. How do I slow down my speech?
Nerves have a lot to answer for. Wanting to get a speech *over and done with* will only result in a gabbled blurt. Rushing also leaves no space for variation of tone or essential rapport building.

The first thing to look at is the length of your speech. Are you struggling to fit it all in? Have you included too much for the time you have allocated? If so, go back through your speech and edit out any unnecessary topics or repeated sentiments.

If the speech is fine but you're still racing then pay attention to your breathing. Make certain you feel grounded and breathe deeply to relax. Try the speech again, slowing down so that the words and images can be received and digested properly by your audience. *NOTE: A well-paced speech is especially important if you're in a room with any sort of echo.*

TASK: (5 mins) Deliver a few lines of your speech, imagining each word as a snowball being thrown too the back of the room. Never throw more than five or six at once. Allow time for these to land before 'throwing' more.

TASK: (5 mins) Imagine you're delivering the speech for the people in the back row who are particularly hard of hearing and rely on lip reading. This will slow you down.

How do I pick up the pace a bit?

If you normally deliver speeches *too slowly* then I suspect you aren't familiar enough with your content. You don't want time to drag or people to disengage whilst you fumble about reading notes or trying to remember what comes next. Dragging a speech or 'buying time' is often a sign of being under-prepared. Really go through your content again and again to ensure you know what's coming next. Alternatively, a speaker can be slow due to nerves - literally struck dumb. If this applies to you then engage your deep breathing, root your feet and focus on the intentions you set out at the beginning, (one of which was to enjoy your speech!) Step 7 is dedicated to the management of fear so don't worry, we will address this more later.

TASK: (5 mins) Practice the speech as an 'Italian run'. This means you speed-speak the entire speech from beginning to end without stopping. It will highlight where your knowledge gaps are and test you on the running order of topics.

TASK: (5 mins) Imagine you have a balloon (or better yet - actually get a balloon) and practice the speed-speech keeping the balloon in the air by hitting it every few words. This will add an extra level of concentration, keep your body engaged and ensure your energy level is up.

I sound a bit boring. How do I sound more interesting?

Keeping the voice energised with *varied intonation* is key if you want to keep your audience engaged. Imagine your voice written down as musical notes. How would they look? Are you creating a symphonic overture …or more of a death march?

Certain accents have a lyrical quality to them already. Southern Irish and many American accents are lyrical and may not need much attention in this area. In the UK, Welsh, Geordie, Cockney and Scottish accents naturally have a wide range of intonation in them already, whereas Birmingham, Mancunian, and Southern Counties accents are flatter and more monotone. Pay attention to your natural accent and see if it would benefit by being adapted.

Storytellers use colour in their voice to paint pictures in the listeners mind. They vary their intonation, speed, pitch and tone regularly and with dramatic effect. Good public speakers also adopt this approach. I encourage you to treat your speech as if it were a story, needing you, the storyteller, to breathe life and energy into it.

TASK: (10 mins) Tell a story about something exciting that has happened to you. Do this out loud and make it as engaging as possible. Think of each sentence as being a 'new thought' with a beginning, middle and end. Imagine you can taste the words in your mouth and that it's your job to make us taste them too. Now practice your speech in exactly the same way and with the same energy.

Another common cause for sounding dreary is going down in pitch or 'dropping off' at the end of words. Many speakers do this without knowing, resulting in the audience not being able to hear or make sense of the sentence. It can also be interpreted as the speaker being disinterested or bored.

TASK: (10 mins) Go through your speech and mark each full stop with a coloured slash (/) This highlights where the end of your sentence actually is. Speak your speech and make a conscious effort not to drop in pitch, driving forwards right up until the slash.

How do I stop myself coming across as uncertain and under-confident?
This may sound harsh but *be more certain*. If you don't know your content well enough then practice more. Remember, confidence comes from preparation.

However if you *are* confident with your content and still coming across as uncertain then you might be doing something linguistically that is being misinterpreted. Are you rising in pitch or 'going up' at the end of a word? We do it naturally when asking a question, but some people fall into the habit of doing this at the end of every sentence. The intention may be to double check the audience is following, but this creates an air of uncertainty and the listener's confidence in the speaker, drops.

TASK: (10 mins) If this is your tendency, listen back to your speech, marking down each time your inflection rises. Read the speech out loud and consciously drop in pitch slightly every time you read these words.

How do I create the 'right' atmosphere for my speech?
Creating the appropriate atmosphere for your speech means looking at the speech's *tone*. What word would you use to describe the intended tone of your overall speech? By this I mean what type of *feeling* or *mood* are you aiming to evoke. Formal? Informal? Inspiring? Jovial?

Tone is created by a combination of many elements and if any of them are incongruent with the intended tone, it throws a spanner in the works and makes something *feel* wrong. This is easily remedied. Think of the qualities your intended tone would have. E.g. A 'welcoming' tone should be warm, inclusive, relaxed and positive. Choose three or four qualities and use them to influence your choice of words and imagery.

TASK: (20 mins) Revisit each area of your speech. Do the words you've chosen match the qualities of your intended tone? Does your voice have the appropriate qualities needed to suit your intended tone? Make any necessary adjustments until each area is congruent with the mood you're hoping to create.
NOTE: Focus on vocal tone at this point. Step 6 concentrates on physical tone.

How do I sound more fluent and less stilted?

If your speech sounds hesitant or you're getting muddled, it may be down to the structure or running order of your content. Be mindful about the *links between* content areas, ensuring they flow relevantly from one to another. However if the speech flows on the page but not on the stage then it's a sign that you don't know it well enough. Achieving a flowing speech will take practice. Keep in mind which topic is coming up next and never start speaking a sentence that you don't know the end of.

TASK: (10 mins) Go through your speech and ensure topics are suitably linked, flowing naturally with relevance to help both you and the listener make sense of it. If you're working from bullet points and getting muddled then consider using a written script.

How do I ensure the important information is heard?

As pointed out in Step 3 a *stress* can give an entirely different meaning to a sentence depending on where it lands. Work out beforehand where the main stress lies within the sentence in order to maximise the message within it.

TASK:

Written speeches. (10 mins) Go through your speech and underline the words that emphasise your message. For example: *I can't tell you how important it is that you actually act upon this advice*

Bullet Points. If you're speaking from bullet points its even more important to know where each sentence is heading in order to add the appropriate stresses as you go along.

How do I appear more (...)?

Apart from highlighting messages, stresses can also be used to change how people *perceive* your communication style. You can adapt the way you speak in order to have a certain impact. This is a useful skill to develop and enables you to tailor your style to best fit your message.

TASK:
If you want to appear **forthright** and **powerful** - *stress all the* ***verbs.***
If you want to appear **methodical** and **factual** - *stress all the* ***nouns.***
If you want to appear **passionate** and **enthusiastic** - *stress all the* ***adjectives.***
If you want to appear **mindful** and **empathic** - *elongate all the vowels*

How do I, (er)…use less…(um, hmmmn) noises? *sigh*
Everyone utters *some* extraneous noises when speaking- it's natural and shows that we're human and not a recording. However when these sounds occur regularly and *unconsciously* they become distracting and even annoying. Feeling nervous, under-prepared, being physically ungrounded or not breathing properly is often the cause. A deep breath and a brief silence is infinitely better than any of these noises.

TASK: (5 mins) Talk for 1-minute non-stop about any topic, the more random the better. Ask a friend to observe this exercise and 'buzz' you if you say *er, um, hmmn* or make any noise they deem as odd or inappropriate. Short pauses or uses of silence are allowed if the listener stills feels comfortable, but they can buzz you if they are *awkward* ones.

Unconscious phrases: It's not just noises that creep unwittingly into our speech. We're all guilty of adding in a word or phrase here or there from time to time. Here are some of the main culprits:

The first word. Even when we have a cracker of a speech planned it's easy to stumble at the first step by speaking before we think. Never start with "Right!" or "Ok!" This is you gearing yourself up to speak and shows that you're not ready. Lead straight in with confidence.

Rushing. Resist any temptation to make a comment about rushing or ending. "I better get on with it" or "Lets get this over with" doesn't set the right tone - even in jest.

The last word. When you reach the end avoid any temptation to signpost it. Never end with "That's it." or "The end." Say 'thank you', accept your applause graciously and leave.

Apologies. Never apologise for lack of preparation. "Sorry, I only found out I was speaking this morning," won't fill your audience with much confidence.

Excuses. No matter how nervous you may feel, never make excuses for your presentation skills. "I'm a bit rubbish at this." Or "This isn't really my thing" is telling the audience you shouldn't be there – and they won't want to be there either.

Over explaining. "I chose this because…" Never over-explain why you've chosen certain content, it should be apparent and wastes valuable rapport-building time.

TASK: Apply all these rules immediately. Practice avoiding these pitfalls when rehearsing your speech in front of others.

How can I use silence more efficiently?
It may feel odd but silence is vital in good communication. There really is no need to *fill the space* when you need time to think. Never underestimate how *comfortable* silence can be if used deliberately and with ease. It's a vital tool that enables your audience to digest what you've said. It allows them time to picture any metaphors or visualise the imagery in the story you're telling.

TASK: Try leaving a brief silence after posing a question to make your audience think. It also gives *you* time to think, gather your thoughts or change direction.

How do I engage more with my audience?

'Engagement' is a human-to-human activity so it's something that can only be practiced in situ – not alone. However, when you *are* in front of an audience the key to engagement is *listening* to them. This might sound strange given you're the one doing all the talking but what I mean is pay attention to the energy in the room. Read them, look at them, listen too them. Are they keeping up? Are they responding to your humour? If they laugh for example then give them space to do so – don't drive forwards over the top of them. Treat your speech like a conversation. Do they appear to be thinking about any questions you pose them? The very act of listening and responding to them will show you acknowledge their presence, respect them and care about the impact you have on them.

NOTE: By reading the audience I don't mean 'try to read their facial expression'. This would be disastrous! Think about your own face when you listen to someone else speaking – do you always sit nodding enthusiastically with an encouraging smile on your face? Neither will they. Listen to the room using your instincts. Also listen to yourself. Hear what you're saying and ensure you're making sense.

TASK: (10 mins) Practice your speech in front of a friend or colleague and take the time to respond to what you're given energetically. Allow space and time to *listen*.

How do I connect passionately with a boring topic?

Not all subject matter is riveting in nature. If you've observed a lack of engagement in your spoken delivery style then it's likely you aren't connecting with your subject matter on a level that's *personal* enough to you. It's easy to talk passionately about interesting topics, but the art of breathing life into a dull topic can transform not only your *speech* but also your *career* and ultimately *your life*.

The key to success is having an <u>authentic</u> approach and bearing in mind these three areas:

There's no such thing as 'Boring'.
This is where most people fall at the first fence and the sooner you grasp this the better. Perception of a topic is *subjective* – everyone is going to have a personalised viewpoint and connection to it. Tax Revenue is riveting to some people. Your own perception of the topic you're speaking about is vital. *How can you expect your audience to be excited by what you're saying if you aren't?*

Using a topic as a springboard into a more passionate place opens up a world of opportunity. So before you deliver a dull speech or fall into the trap of whitewashing a 'boring' topic with fake enthusiasm and tenuous selling points (that audiences can smell a mile off) take a moment to remember *there's no such thing as boring.*

It's all about <u>you.</u>
You may have been told public speaking is all about your audience but believe me *this* is the secret everyone is missing: <u>at this point it's all about you.</u> All audiences need a doorway into *any* speech, exciting or not. Before the speech begins it's a 'you and them' situation. They're in the audience and you're standing in front of them. They have no *active* connection, personal or otherwise to what you are about to say so the key to success here is *you*. You're the gatekeeper into this passionate Kingdom of fascinating facts, stories and inspirational energy. You're Willy Wonka welcoming them at the gates of the chocolate factory.

And here's the Golden Ticket – you must use *Knowledge & Passion Pools* ™ to deeply connect with your subject on a personal level.

The object here is to find parallels between what you *are* knowledgeable and passionate about and simply <u>link these energised stories and facts with your current speech topic.</u>

Knowledge & Passion Pools™ are topics you're personally passionate and knowledgeable about. It could be people, places, travel, education, children, art, sport, history, civil rights – anything you could talk about for a few minutes with passion, knowledge and authenticity. These are your go-to areas – your passion pools - to inject life and energy into your speech. Only once you've inspired your audience through your own dynamic, personal connection to your subject can you really consider their needs.

<u>*Now* it's all about them.</u>
With your audience engaged it's now time to address *their* hopes and needs. What are they hoping, wanting and needing to hear from you? From this point onwards, tailor your message (the reason you're standing before them right now) and subject matter to suit *their* agenda. Always keep your objective (what you want them to go away feeling, thinking or doing as a result of watching your speech) in the back of your mind to keep you on track.

Now both you and your audience are passionately connected to the seemingly 'boring' topic at an energised and personal level

TASK: (15 mins) Fill your knowledge & passion pools.
Choose a subject you are passionate about. Practice talking about it for 5 minutes non-stop. Use as many vibrant stories, facts and examples as possible. Repeat this with 2 further subjects. Practice dipping into these 3 knowledge & passion pools regularly – the day may arrive when they come to your rescue!

TASK: (30 mins) Practice linking your knowledge & passion pools to a dull subject. Pick a random topic you know little about. Imagine a scenario where you could be giving a speech about this subject. Give yourself 10 minutes to prepare and deliver a passionate speech that links it to your knowledge and passion pools. Try googling an interesting fact or inspirational quote related to your topic and add it in.

By the end of Step 5 you have the means to:

Be loud enough.
Be clear enough.
Be well paced.
Speak with breath control and support.
Deliver with an appropriate tone.
Adopt a storytelling approach using varied intonation and inflections.
Connect with your subject matter personally and passionately.
Highlight your message with effective use of stresses.
Listen and respond to your audience.
Reduce unnecessary 'ums/ers/hmmns'.
Feel confident with pauses and silence.
Deliver fluently in style and content.

Move on to Step 6

Step 6: Delivery Technique (Physical)

> *Your body language, your eyes, your energy will come through*
> *to your audience before you even start speaking.*
> *Peter Guber*

This step addresses any physical issues that have arisen and covers body language, gesture, facial expression, entrances and exits. Refer to your list once again and work through each area until you feel confident physically.

Does my physicality really matter?
Definitely. You are never *not* communicating. Remember, a vast amount of communication is non-verbal, so what you're doing physically is going to be interpreted by your audience whether you want them to or not. Looking confident physically is also going to *strengthen your audience connection.* They'll feel safe and comfortable in your presence, trusting that you know what you're talking about.

How do I enter the space?
Your speech begins the moment you set foot 'onstage'. This is not the time to be looking at notes, practicing opening sentences or straightening your clothing. When your mental and physical preparation has been sufficiently invested in, you'll *enjoy* stepping onto the stage instead of dreading it. Simply take a few deep breaths and head out there with a smile, ready to make eye contact with people as soon as you can.

How should I stand?
Once you've arrived at your spot or podium take the time you need to find a comfortable stance.

Neutral Stance - A neutral stance with weight equally distributed will help keep you grounded and avoid nervous swaying, pacing, foot tapping or sitting in hips. Imagine breathing into your feet and allow your weight to drop downwards. Relax your arms and imagine a string tied to the top of your head, gently pulling you up straight.

Use this as your default stance. It may feel unusual or exposing at first, as your body fights to protect itself with fidgets and awkward tension, but keep breathing and in a few seconds you'll feel more comfortable and grounded. From this centred place you'll notice movements and gestures happen naturally without feeling forced or premeditated.

TASK: (5 mins) Practice entering the space. This might seem silly but *fear of the unknown* is what we're eliminating here. Do this in the actual venue if possible or if there's time before you speak. By doing this it won't feel so alien on the day itself. Climb the stairs, walk over to your speaker position and stand there in neutral for a few minutes. Get comfy and familiar. If you don't have access to the space itself then practice your entrance elsewhere and *imagine* you're there. It's amazing what a difference this can make.

How do I use my body to engage with everybody in the room?
The key to audience engagement is making each member feel like you're speaking directly to them. Making the effort to reach each area of the audience with firm eye contact will help people feel included and connect to you and your topic.

TASK: (5 mins) Stand at one end of the room, take a deep breath and visualise the space you'll be speaking in. See it in as much detail as possible. Draw it out in your mind. How close will the front row be? How far away is the back row? How wide will the rows be? Is there a balcony above? Practice turning your head to look at each of the four corners. Look straight ahead, holding your arms out to the side with your palms facing forwards (like a big hug) and without moving either your head or eyes use your peripheral vision to see the entire room. Set the intention to include the entire room at all times.

Lets call this 'holding the space.' It's a powerful sensation and a technique used by theatre actors and politicians.

When addressing larger audiences it's impossible to make actual eye contact with each individual. That would be exhausting, highly distracting and result in unfocused 'eye-flitting'. What we're aiming to achieve here is the *impression* that you're making personal eye contact.

TASK: (10 mins) Recite your speech, directing each new sentence to a different corner of the auditorium. Add in your 'holding the space' position. Once you've done that a few times start directing each new sentence to other areas of the room.
NOTE: Notice how easy it is to let eye contact drift mid-sentence or waft aimlessly. <u>Do not let this happen. Choose an area and stick to it.</u>

A final note on eye contact – if you're using notes, be aware how repeatedly glancing down may break your concentration and also you audience's. For this reason alone it is worth *learning your speech by heart, or being solid with the content of each bulleted topic.*

How can I appear more relaxed?
No one enjoys watching a tense speaker. It's too painful. This is because it's human nature to mirror other people, so if they laugh – we laugh, if they get upset - we get upset, if they're tense and nervous – we get tense and nervous too.

The way to appear more relaxed is to *be* more relaxed. Feeling confident on the inside is the key to appearing confident on the outside. Simple preparations before you speak can help. I can't tell you exactly how to be relaxed – your task is to find out what elements contribute to that. Apart from being confident with the content of your speech it could be having a hot drink beforehand or wearing something comfortable that doesn't show sweat patches.

Give it some thought. What would create a relaxing atmosphere for you?

These suggestions will certainly help:

DON'T drink alcohol beforehand. A quick dram to steady the nerves can often have the opposite affect and enhance them.
DON'T drink large amounts of coffee or stimulants immediately beforehand. It can heighten nerves and stop you from relaxing.
DON'T make too may jokes during your speech. It might be your intention to 'break the ice' but if they aren't well received you'll end up feeling tense.

DO *practice your speech*. Feeling prepared is the best way to be relaxed. Do it out loud as many times as you need in the days leading up to it.
DO practice your speech looking directly into someone's eyes. Experiencing this will stop it feeling distracting on the day.
DO smile! Obvious, I know, but don't take this advice lightly. It's the first thing to go out the window when nerves arrive. The act of smiling helps the body to relax. It also encourages the audience to enjoy our presence and relax themselves.
DO breathe! Having enough oxygen in your system will keep nerves at bay and help you relax. When we tense up we restrict our ability to breath and usually take shorter, quicker, ineffective breaths. Consciously taking deeper, slower breaths will prevent the sensation of panic or anxiety.

What should I be doing with my arms and hands?
Arms can end up having a life of their own. Knowing what your habits are and how an audience perceives them may help you to adapt and maintain a more neutral position:

Gesture (hand and arm)
Flapping. This can be perceived as being flippant or frustrated.

Wafting. This feels like your arm is moving on its' own. It gives the impression of uncertainty or insecurity.

Clenching. The clenching and releasing of hands shows anxiety and tension. It can also make you look angry.

Fiddling. Pulling at clothes, flicking hair, twisting rings or watches, fiddling with fingers, pens, notes or glasses shows nerves and is distracting for the audience.

Punching. Punching your palm (or the air) with your fist to get a point across may feel powerful but is often perceived as being frustrated and weak.

Wringing. The twisting of hands, clothes or indeed just using a wringing gesture makes a speaker appear untrustworthy or manipulative.

Slicing. Like punching, the use of a slicing gesture can be perceived as being frustrated or desperate.

Shrugging. Is perceived as non-committal or uncertain.

Pointing. This can come across as patronising or overbearing.

TASK: (10 mins) If you find any of these gestures regularly cropping-up in your recording then practice keeping your hands softly held together. Allow a gesture only when it feels natural and generally keep the palms facing upwards. Alternatively try holding something like a pen or cue card – a prop often adds a sense of security.

NOTE: Watch some TED talks on youtube. You'll see hundreds of ways to give effective speeches with minimal movement and just a few relaxed gestures.

Should I stand still or can I move about?
Moving is fine if the movement has come from an impulse to address a different area of the room. Watch out for these habits:

Pacing. Aimless wandering or nervous pacing comes from not being grounded enough. If in doubt stand in neutral stance and feel your weight against the ground.

Tapping. Along with scuffing or dragging your feet, tapping shows nerves and anxiety.

Swaying. This makes a speaker look uncomfortable or uncertain.

Bouncing. Bobbing up and down on your toes comes across as nerves but is often a sign that you have energy, eager to get out. This isn't always a bad thing. Try moving to another area of the stage to channel it and then return to neutral stance.

TASK: (20 mins) Give your speech in neutral stance from beginning to end. Once you've mastered it repeat the speech and allow yourself no more than 3 moves. Make certain these moves are deliberate and finish in a grounded, neutral stance.

What should I do with my head?

The position of your head directs your focus and attention. It also directs your audience's focus and attention. In short, they look where you look. Be conscious of this and make the effort to include each area of the audience slowly without flitting about. Head actions to avoid are:

Jutting. People with a tendency to jut their head forwards can be perceived as being aggressive and pushy.

Angles. Not all angles are bad, but an over-use of 'empathically' tipping your head to one side comes across as patronising or uncertain.

Nodding. Repeatedly nodding is very distracting for an audience. It looks a bit desperate and insecure.

TASK: (5 mins) Deliver the first few lines of your speech imagining that your head is a bowling ball on a plate of oil. Allow it to move smoothly.

How should I use facial expression?

Our facial expressions are always going to be interpreted by an audience. Be conscious of any habits, such as:

Frowning. Comes across as severe.

Overactive eyebrows. Perceived as desperate.

Blank face. Can read as being bored, unengaged or nervous.

Overly expressive. Pulling too many faces can come across as insecurity.

Lip biting. Quite obviously looks like nerves.

Wincing or Gurning. This is the facial equivalent of a shrug. It's perceived as uncertainty.

TASK: (10 mins) Practice speaking with a neutral face. This doesn't mean a blank expression. It's a gentle smile that softens the face and engages the facial muscles enough to discourage overactive expression.

What if I'm giving my speech sitting down?

If your speech is given sitting down then all previous advice still applies. Also be aware of:

Slouching. This is a submissive state and is perceived as not caring, not engaging or feeling defeated.

Crossed arms. This self-protecting gesture shows insecurity.

Inverted legs. Again this shows insecurity.

Slumping on a table. This is too informal and comes across as being disinterested.

Leg swinging. This shows anxiety, low status and is distracting to the audience.

Leg crossing. Despite being a 'closed' position, leg crossing is considered acceptable if accompanied by a relaxed upper body. Avoid combining leg crossing with arm folding or body hugging.

TASK: (5 mins) Develop an upright neutral sitting stance where your weight is directly above the sitting bones and the core of the body engaged. Relax your arms. It's possible to sit like this and still cross your legs.

What does effective body language look like?

Undoubtedly, the more *relaxed* a speaker feels the more effective their body language will be – because it will come naturally. Note that relaxed does not mean collapsed, it is engaged and energised yet holds no unnecessary tension. A grounded stance and neutral facial expression is a great default to work from. It allows you to feel relaxed and let through your natural personality.

Power stances. According to Amy Cuddy's 'most watched' TED talk, *Your body language shapes who you are,* the use of power stances can not only effect how people perceive you but also result in chemical changes in your body. By adopting a more open stance for as little as two minutes the level of testosterone (the dominance chemical) in the body rises by approximately 20% and levels of cortisol (the stress chemical) goes down by 25%.

TASK: (2 mins) Before practicing your speech, stand for two minutes with your hands on your hips and legs apart, or with your arms in a 'victorious' V above your head. See if it makes a difference to your confidence and the way you present. If so, do this in the bathroom before your speech on the day. It might look silly, but no one else will see and if it gets results it will be worth it.

How do I appear more 'authentic'?

With so much to think about it's easy to get overwhelmed by the task in hand and approach the event in a 'public speaking by numbers' sort of way. Being authentic requires you to stay rooted in your body and not be swept away by the chatter inside your head. You need to be connected to your breath, grounded through your feet and to release all unnecessary tension. Have absolute trust that your preparation will serve you well. Stick to your key message and objective at all times and do all you can to connect with your audience. Aim to achieve your 5 core intentions drawn up in Step 1, breathe deeply throughout, *be yourself* and above all – *enjoy* yourself.

How do I leave the stage?

How you finish your speech and exit the stage is easy to overlook. Don't. This is the last thing people will remember. End with an upbeat 'thank you' and don't be eager to run off. Accept any applause graciously with a smile and eye contact with each four corners. Take any notes or props with you and exit with confidence. Remember, if your speech starts the second you set foot onstage – then it's not over until the second you step off it.

TASK: (5 mins) Practice the last few sentences of your speech and how you will exit the stage. Do this 3 times.

Should I incorporate handouts and technical equipment into my speech?

Slides, Overhead Projectors and PowerPoint. Adding visuals to your presentation can enhance it by adding a new dimension. Pictures, graphs, quotes and selective information enables your audience to gain further insight into your topic and gives those with a more visual mind a chance to engage.

Make certain any visual you use adds something to your speech, there's no point in putting up a list and reading through it – that's just doubling up. If you have a visual list of bullet points then be sure to embellish on what's written to add something further.

Stay clear of 'gimmick pictures' that have little to do with the core message of your speech – this confuses the audience. They'll spend their time trying to figure out why its there instead of listening to you.

Stand to the side of any screens so you can gesture towards it without having to turn upstage or break eye contact. I suggest investing in an automatic remote control. This enables you to remain facing the audience at all times. This is very important as turning away can allow your audience to disengage immediately. Having a remote also gives you something to hold on to, stopping you making unnecessary gestures or fidgeting.

NOTE: Test all equipment before you speak to avoid embarrassing technical hitches.

Handouts. Avoid giving handouts before a speech as this makes people look down to read instead of listen to you. Give them out at the end.

Visuals in general. Don't use visuals as an alternative opportunity to info-dump. Be selective and only include information that is completely relevant. As a rule it's always best to ask yourself *is this absolutely necessary* when considering the use of pictures and extra equipment. If it isn't then don't. What doesn't add only detracts.

At the end of Step 6 you have learned:
How to enter the space.
How to stand neutrally.
How to engage your audience with eye contact.
How to appear more relaxed.
How to eliminate bad physical traits.
How to appear more powerful and authentic.
How to exit the stage.

Move on to Step 7

Step 7: Dealing with nerves

> *'Fear is excitement without breath.'*
> *Robert Heller*

Coping with nerves is often the primary reason people seek help. So why wait until Step 7 before addressing it? Because *being under-prepared* is the main culprit for nerves and fear - so congratulations - by completing Steps 1-6 you are far from under-prepared.

It's important for you to acknowledge the work you've put in by this stage, trusting the quality of the speech itself, the skills you've picked up, physically and vocally, and focus now on your original set of core intentions. The hard work is done and delivering the speech should now be an enjoyable experience. Remember, *there is no room for self-doubt in public speaking.* Trust your preparation.

All that said, it would be foolish to ignore the fact that sometimes nerves will arise. This is perfectly natural. Public speaking by its very nature is a venture into the unknown. *Who will be in the audience? What mood will they be in? Will I remember everything?* Putting ourselves into an unfamiliar situation that we perceive to be threatening triggers our 'flight or fight' response. This starts a chain reaction in our brain that results in body tension, a faster heart rate and a surge of adrenaline. Therefore by completing steps 1-6 you have dramatically reduced the 'unknown'.

How can I deal with nerves and enjoy speaking more?

The sensations we experience when fearful are the same as when we're excited - only we perceive them as being negative. By seeing this energy as a *positive* thing we can harness the adrenaline and put it to good use by adding controlled breath. Breathe deeply and unlock the tension to diffuse the anxiety and flood the body with a more pleasant sensation. Turn butterflies in the stomach into bubbles of excitement. Remind yourself that you are fully prepared and ready to speak. *Fear is fuel.*

Follow the exercises below to manage anxiety and eliminate nerves. They have been split into three sections:

Section 1: During Preparation
Section 2: The moment before you speak
Section 3: During the speech itself

Section 1: During preparation:
Challenge any fears you have. Worrying about what *could* happen is a wasted energy. The majority of these scenarios never arise. Any previous bad experiences should have been worked through in Step 1, providing you with essential knowledge of why it happened and how to deal with that event in the future.

TASK: (15 mins) Ask yourself 'what's the worst that can happen?' Write each scenario down. Now come up with a Plan B - think about how you could prevent this situation from occurring or deal with it, should it arise.

Section 2: Before you speak:
Keep Breathing. In the moments leading up to your speech make a conscious effort to keep breathing deep, even breaths. Picture the air flooding your body with a calming colour. Imagine sending the breath right down into your feet.

Normalise a racing heartbeat. If you feel anxiety rising and notice your heartbeat racing try reining it back in with 3 quick breaths follow by 3 slow, deep ones. The surge of oxygen will leave you feeling calmer.

Blow on your thumb. Take a deep breath and blow on your thumb making the breath last as long as you can. This really does work!

Yawn. Force yourself to do a big yawn. It provides oxygen, relaxes the body and throat muscles. Be sure to do this in private so as not to appear disinterested!

Drink water. VERY IMPORTANT. Dehydration is an awful feeling. It's a distraction no speaker wants and stops you thinking and speaking clearly. Drink plenty of water (not caffeine or alcohol) in the hours leading up to your speech. Keep a bottle of water with you. It doesn't hurt to have water on the stage.

Exercise. Many successful speakers find exercising a huge benefit. It awakens the body, lungs and brain. Try a gym session, run or brisk walk earlier in the day, or a few sit-ups and stretches before the actual speech itself.

Smile. Send relaxing signals to the brain by smiling in the minutes leading up to your speech.

Bathroom. Be sure to use the bathroom with plenty of time to spare. Feeling to need to nip to the toilet seconds before you get up on stage does no good to anyone's focus.

Talk with the audience beforehand. If the opportunity to speak to members of your audience beforehand is there – take it. They'll engage more with you during your speech and you'll relax in the process. It's always nicer to talk to people you feel you know already.

Keep perspective. Remind yourself - this is not heart surgery, people do MUCH more daring and dangerous things than this. Keep perspective. You'll be fine no matter what.

Section 3: During the speech:
Smile. Again, keep smiling for the stress-relieving benefits but also to encourage audience engagement.

Imagery. Many people use imagery and visualisation to help deal with nerves whilst up on stage. Personally I've never found this technique works – namely because I'm far too occupied with the speech itself. This is not to say, however, that the technique won't work for you. Options include picturing yourself somewhere relaxing like on a beach or the old favourite of imagining everyone naked to amuse and relax you. Like I say, it's never worked for me but have a go if it appeals.

Pauses & Breaths. In the heat of the moment my go-to technique for dealing with nerves is always the simplest. After finishing a piece of content take a brief moment to pause, breathe and gather yourself before beginning your next section. It acts as a reset button if you will, allowing time for the audience to digest what you've just talked about and ready themselves for the next part. People are surprisingly comfortable with pauses and silence, so don't worry. It need be no more than a few seconds.

Serve your audience. Remember its *ultimately* not all about you – its about your audience. If you're starting to panic then reset your intention to *enjoy providing the audience with the information they need*. You are helping them. Turn the focus back outwards.

Welcome in the unexpected. Some of the most memorable and wonderful moments come as a direct result of something unexpected. By being overly rigid you could miss out on impromptu profound moments. Make a conscious decision to embrace the uncertainty of the unknown.

And there you have it. By following Steps 1-7 you now have everything you need to deliver Panic-Free, engaging, dynamic and well-rounded speeches with confidence.

You're now ready to give your speech. Enjoy it.

Consolidation Exercises

These final tips and exercises are here to ensure your skills continue to develop, bed-in and serve you throughout your professional life and outside it too.

Practice makes perfect. In this case it really does. The more experience we get the better. Don't shy away from opportunities to stand up in front of others and keep your new skills polished.

TASK: (30 mins) Practice a new speech with colleagues or friends and invite some fresh feedback. Remember to be specific about the areas of feedback you're looking for

Re-film yourself. I'm sure you'll be amazed at the difference – but remember the biggest improvement has happened *inside*. People always feel more nervous than they look. Being able to deliver with confidence and having knowledge of how to handle anxiety is a massive achievement in itself.

TASK: (30 mins) Get back in front of the camera and re-film your presentation. Refer back to your list of self-analysed observations from Step 2. What can you tick off the list? What areas could do with some further work?

Seek professional help for persistent linguistic needs. If during your journey you have uncovered some persistent vocal hurdles then don't be afraid to seek specific advice and training from a linguistic professional. Any vocal coach worthy of the name will be able to address your needs with one-to-one sessions, giving you exercises to correct the issue or coping mechanisms to lessen the impact on your speech. Be sure to research beforehand and choose someone with valid testimonials from satisfied clients.

Use every opportunity. Don't pack these skills away once your speech is over and done. The techniques you've worked hard to learn and develop will serve you in every aspect of life. Nurture them with passion and enjoy the knowledge that you have a skill that inspires others.

TASK: (2 mins) Each week practice talking non-stop for 2 minutes on one of your Passion/Knowledge Pools.

TASK: (15 mins) Choose a topic right now, give yourself 10 minutes to prepare and deliver a 5 minute speech. Don't think about it – just go for it!

Top-Tips at a Glance:

Use the list below as a swift reminder before delivering your speech.

- Ensure your speech includes your message, your objective and considers your audience's needs.
- Warm up properly before you speak.
- Breathe deep, even breaths to help ground your feet, relax your body and support your voice.
- Know your content (and links) back to front.
- Always practice out loud.
- Think of yourself as a storyteller. Use varied inflection, intonation, pitch and speed.
- Connect with your topic on a personal level.
- Use stress effectively to highlight your message.
- Never apologise, explain or excuse.
- Don't be afraid to use silence and pauses.
- Listen to your audience.
- Your speech starts the moment you set foot on stage.
- Your speech doesn't finish until you step off stage.
- Use eye contact with confidence, addressing each area of the space.
- Smile.
- Trust your preparation.
- Focus on achieving your *5 core objectives*.
- Drink plenty of water.
- Serve your audience's needs.
- Keep perspective. You'll be fine whatever happens.

I hope you've enjoyed this Panic-Free Public Speaking Book and felt the benefit from each practical task. Get out there and *enjoy* serving your audience by delivering your message with confidence in a way that will benefit both them and you. Let me know how you get on!

Best wishes,
Edward London-Lane.

Liked this book? Please leave a review on www.amazon.com or www.amazon.co.uk

@EdLondonLane

Printed in Great
Britain
by Amazon